To _____

_____

From _____

Date _____

First edition

Published by Ladybird Books Ltd Loughborough Leicestershire UK
Ladybird Books Inc Auburn Maine 04210 USA

Printed in England

The Ladybird
Baby Book
A record of baby's early years

compiled by LIS COLLINS
illustrated by SARAH ROSS

Ladybird Books

Monday's child is fair of face,
Tuesday's child is full of grace,
Wednesday's child is full of woe,
Thursday's child has far to go,
Friday's child is loving and giving,
Saturday's child works hard
                    for a living,
And the child that is born
                    on the Sabbath day,
Is fair and wise and good and gay.

Baby

name

. . . .

date due

. . . .

date of arrival

. . . .

day of birth

. . . .

time of birth

. . . .

birthplace

. . . .

doctor

. . . .

midwife/nurse

. . . .

About me

My measurements

age	height	weight
. . . .	. . . .	. . . .
. . . .	. . . .	. . . .
. . . .	. . . .	. . . .
. . . .	. . . .	. . . .
. . . .	. . . .	. . . .

hospital name bracelet   *lock of hair*

colour of eyes

....

amount of hair

....

resemblances

....

outline of baby's hand

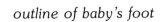

outline of baby's foot

When baby was born

popular songs

. . . .

. . . .

big names in sport

. . . .

. . . .

popular television series

. . . .

. . . .

best film of the year

. . . .

newspaper headlines

....

....

political figures

....

....

fashions

....

....

Milestones

first slept through the night

....

took solid food

....

cut first tooth

....

sat up alone

....

crawled

....

stood alone

....

took first steps

....

spoke first word

....

My favourite things

toys . . . .
. . . .
games . . . .
. . . .
stories . . . .
. . . .
songs/rhymes . . . .
. . . .

food . . . .
. . . .
animals . . . .
. . . .
friends . . . .
. . . .
special interests . . . .
. . . .

My special words

for family . . . .
. . . .

for friends . . . .
. . . .

for animals . . . .
. . . .

for toys . . . .
. . . .

for other things
. . . .
. . . .
. . . .
. . . .

My early mischief

comments . . . .
. . . .
. . . .
. . . .
. . . .
. . . .
. . . .
. . . .

First Christmas

comments . . . .
. . . .
. . . .
. . . .
. . . .
. . . .

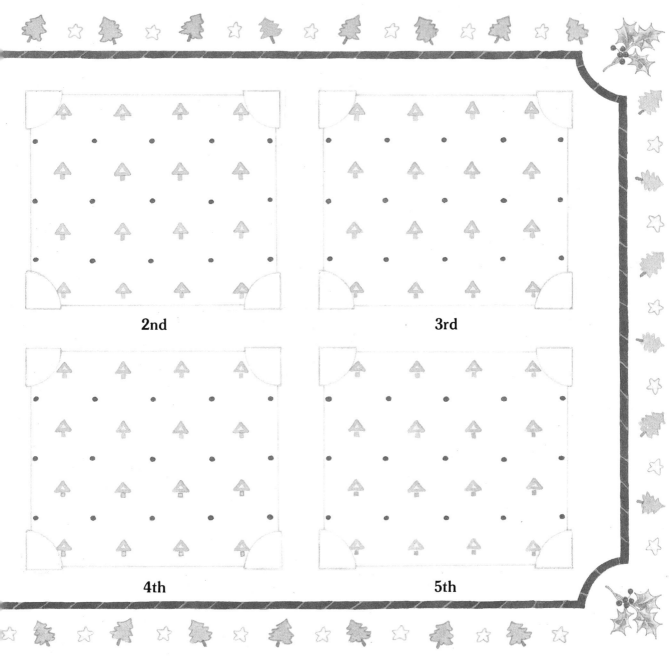

2nd

3rd

4th

5th

First Birthday

comments . . . .

. . . .

. . . .

. . . .

. . . .

Holidays and outings

Playgroup

name of playgroup

....

first day

....

teacher's name

....

new friends

....

....

....

My first drawing

title of picture... *age*............

Starting school

name of school

. . . .

first day

. . . .

teacher's name

. . . .

new friends . . . .

. . . .

My first writing

Pictures of me

Medical record

Immunisation / Vaccination	Age	Date
Triple vaccine (DTP) Diphtheria, Tetanus, Whooping cough 1st	From 3 months	. . . .
Poliomyelitis drops 1st		. . . .
DTP 2nd	5-6 months	. . . .
Poliomyelitis drops 2nd		. . . .
DTP 3rd	10-13 months	. . . .
Poliomyelitis drops 3rd		. . . .
Measles or Measles, Mumps, Rubella (MMR) vaccine	13-15 months	. . . .
Diphtheria booster	4-5 years	. . . .
Tetanus booster		. . . .
Poliomyelitis booster		. . . .
MMR (if not given at 13-15 months)		. . . .